Make it ea

English

Age 5–6

Lynn Huggins-Cooper

Rhyming words

Look at this sentence. All the words in bold rhyme. That means they contain the **same sound**. They all end in the letters *at*.

The **fat cat sat** on the **mat**, watching a **bat**!

I Draw a line to join each word with its rhyme partner.

a can	red
b pink	sack
c bug	dot
d bed	stink
e pot	plug
f back	fan

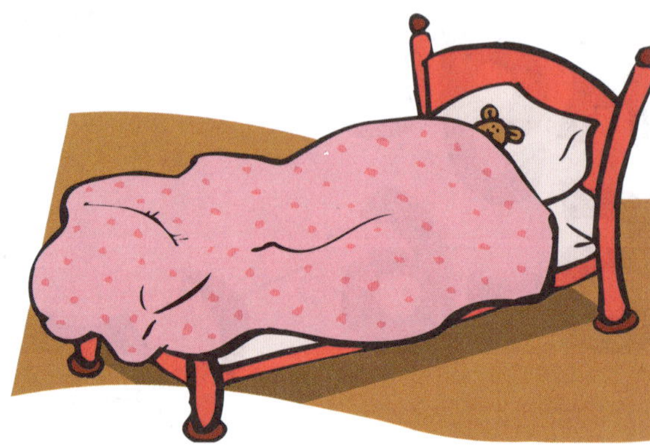

II Look in the box to find words that rhyme with each word below. Write the words in the blank spaces.

a yell __________

b dark __________

c dog __________

d box __________

e win __________

f sock __________

g big __________

fox
frog
pig
smell
rock
bin
park

The alphabet

a b c d e f g h i j k l m n o p q r s t u v w x y z

When people say words are in **alphabetical order** it means they appear in the same order as the alphabet. **A** words come first, then **b** words right up until the end of the alphabet.

bat zebra ant put into alphabetical order is **ant bat zebra**.

I Write these letters in alphabetical order.

a f b a d c e g ______________________

b z x y w v u ______________________

c p r q t s u v ______________________

d g f i h k j m l ______________________

e m l n k j o p ______________________

f s t v u w r x ______________________

g d f e h i g j k ______________________

II Write each set of words in alphabetical order.

a cat egg box ______________________

b bag dig apple ______________________

c cup art pig ______________________

d car baby dog ______________________

e wall bed door ______________________

f book sun leg ______________________

g tree bird peg ______________________

Spelling simple words

Learning to spell is easy when you use:
look, cover, write, check.

First **look** at the word. Look to see if there are any letters with tails that hang below the line, or sticks that 'stick up' above the line. Try to see the word in your head.

Then **cover** the word up and try to **write** it. Uncover the word and **check** it. See if you were right. Keep practising!

I Learn these words. Use look, cover, write, check.

a saw
b say
c now
d yes
e did
f not
g was
h but
i run

II Add the missing letter to each word. Use the letters in the box to help you.

a m___n 

b f___n 

c p___g 

d p___n 

a i o u

e d___t 

f w___g 

g s___n 

h b___ll 

Writing practice

It is important to **write neatly**, so that people can read your writing. Before you start, make sure you are sitting comfortably and you are holding your pencil in the right way between your finger and thumb.

I Trace over these words.

a way us to

b too how her

c him old one

d or out saw

e so not now

II Copy each word three times.

a see ______ ______ ______

b ran ______ ______ ______

c our ______ ______ ______

d pot ______ ______ ______

e that ______ ______ ______

Full stops and capital letters

A sentence always **starts** with a capital letter and most sentences **end** with a full stop.

It is hot today.

capital letter (It) — full stop (.)

I Write these sentences again, adding capital letters and full stops.

a i like you ______

b this is my sister ______

c sausages are my favourite ______

d i am going out ______

e i want to read ______

II These sentences are mixed up. Write them out in the right order. Use a capital letter and a full stop in each sentence.

a like brother i my

______

b dog my walking likes

______

c smell the cat food can its

______

d eat we sweets

______

e wet makes rain you

______

Names

The name of a **person** or **place** should **start** with a capital letter.

*My cat is called **W**iggy.*

*I come from **B**righton.*

I Circle the letters that should be capitals.

a brian

b mrs jones

c andrew

d england

e mr brown

f miss lacey

g london

h mr smith

i france

j janet

k doctor doolittle

l cambridge

m africa

n scotland

II Now underline all of the letters that should be capitals in these sentences. Do not forget to add the full stops!

a my friend jamila comes from yorkshire

b my dog is called bertie

c auntie jane lives in edinburgh

d bruce, stella and jodi are my friends

e we sailed down the river thames

f dad's name is john

g i am going on holiday to portugal with my sister sarah

h i went to durham to see the pantomime cinderella

ff words

Words are made when letters and groups of letters are put together. Learning the way that groups of letters are put together helps you to **build new words.**

o + *f* = o*f* **o + *ff* = o*ff***

The two *ff*s sound different to one *f* on its own.

I

Look at these letters and groups of letters. Write the words they make in the puffs of smoke.

a flu + ff =

b pu + ff =

c bu + ff =

d cu + ff =

e sni + ff =

f sti + ff =

g mu + ff =

h stu + ff =

i sta + ff =

j whi + ff =

II

Write the correct *ff* word next to each picture. Use the words in the box to help you.

muff	cliff	giraffe	puff	whiff	sniff

a  ____________

b  ____________

c  ____________

d  ____________

e  ____________

f  ____________

ll words

Some words end in *ll*. These letters always have a vowel in front of them.

a e i o u

tall

I Make words using the endings in the ball.

a b*all bull bill bell*

b y________________

c s________________

d c________________

e h________________

f d________________

g f________________

h p________________

i t________________

j w________________

II Write the *ll* word for each picture.

a

___ ___ ___ ___

c

___ ___ ___ ___

e

___ ___ ___ ___

b

___ ___ ___ ___

d

___ ___ ___ ___

f

___ ___ ___ ___

ss words

Some words end in *ss*.

cro**ss**

*flo***ss**

I Join the *ss* word to the right picture.

a address

b chess

c pass

d dress

e cress

f floss

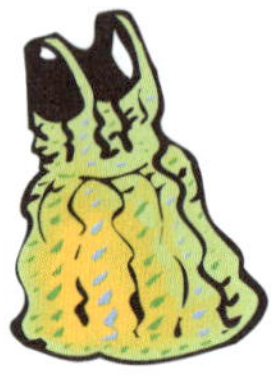

II Choose an *ss* word from the box to complete each sentence.

hiss	floss	mess	grass	kiss	cress

a I sat on the ________________.

b The mud made a ________________.

c I like egg and ________________ sandwiches.

d Candy ________________ is sweet!

e I ________________ my granny.

f The snake went ________________.

ck words

In English a word **never starts** with *ck*. But sometimes *ck* is found in the middle or at the end of a word.

I Draw a picture for each *ck* word.

a clock

b block

c sock

d rocket

e lock

f duck

II *ick* or *ock*? Add the letters to complete the words. Some words can use both – but can you say which ones?

a s ick sock

b kn__________

c w__________

d fl__________

e p__________

f r__________

g l__________

h st__________

i sm__________

j tr__________

ng words

The letter blend *ng* never appears at the beginning of words. It is found at the **end** or in the **middle**.

I Circle the words that use *ng*.

a square rectangle circle

b apple lemon orange

c monkey orangutan ape

d sing laugh shout

e queen prince king

f triangle cymbal drum

g penguin walrus seal

h swing slide roundabout

i necklace ring bracelet

j finger thumb hand

k sting hurt burn

l herring cod eel

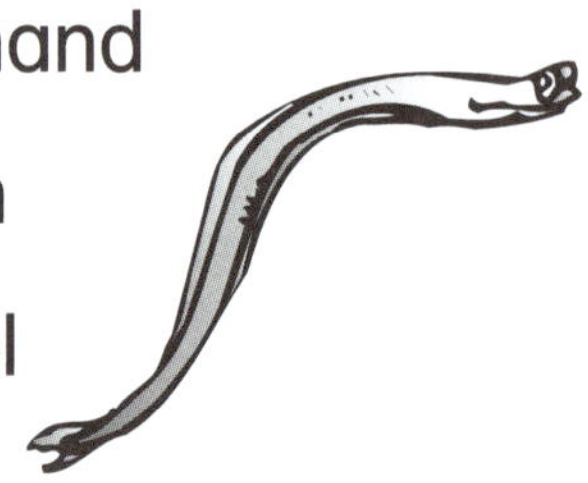

II Write a sentence using each *ing* word.

a cooking ______________________________

____

b running ______________________________

____

c calling ______________________________

____

d shouting ______________________________

____

e looking ______________________________

____

bl words

b and *l* make the letter blend *bl*. Lots of words **start** with *bl*.

blew

bloom

I Tick the words that start with the blend *bl*.

a back dark bland

b black bright big

c baby bin blue

d blend bark brave

e bus blank broom

f bleat bran bill

g burn bleep ball

h bloat bunny barn

i brand bit bleak

j blade brass bust

II Draw a picture for each *bl* word. This will show that you know what it means.

a blade

b blink

c blow

d blue

e blast

cr words

The letters *c* and *r* blend together at the beginning of words to make the sound *cr*.

I Draw a line to match each picture to the correct *cr* word.

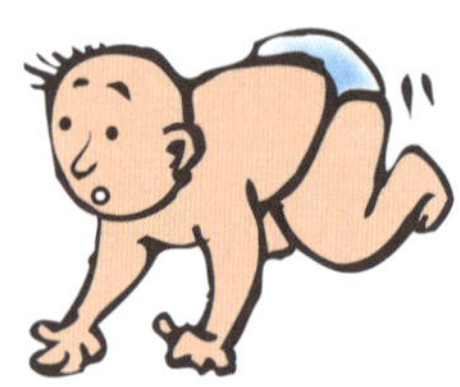

a crab

b cross

c crisp

d crib

e cress

f crawl

g cry

h crust

II Draw a picture that contains each of the things described by these *cr* words.

a crack **b** crane **c** crazy **d** crawl

tr words

Lots of words **start** with the letter blend *tr*.

trumpet

truck

I Find the *tr* words in the box below. Then write them down.

take trade tick tramp trash table travel tray
telly trip tank true trumpet

a ______________ e ______________

b ______________ f ______________

c ______________ g ______________

d ______________ h ______________

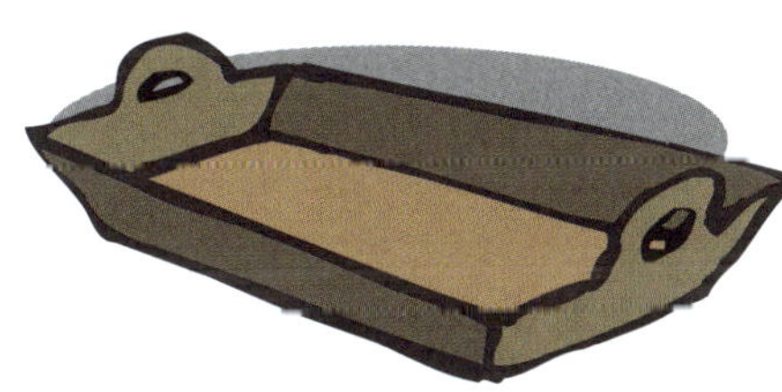

II Write the correct *tr* words in the spaces.

tree
track
train
tractor
try
trap
traffic

a I walked down the ______________.

b The farmer drives a ______________.

c I went to my grandad's house on a ______________.

d The fly was caught in the spider's ______________.

e When you cross the road, watch for ______________.

f The bird made a nest in a ______________.

g I always ______________ my best.

str words

Sometimes blends are made from more than two letters. *S*, *t* and *r* are put together to make the blend *str*. You find it at the beginning of many words.

I **Circle the word that begins with *str*.**

a strap soft sell

b stall string stink

c strong sand sit

d save street sell

e straw sold saw

f seen so stream

g sick sit stretch

h strange silly smell

II **Now write a sentence using each word you circled.**

a ______________________

b ______________________

c ______________________

d ______________________

e ______________________

f ______________________

g ______________________

h ______________________

nd and *lp* words

lp and *nd* are letter blends found at the **end of words**. Like *ck* and *ng*, they never appear at the beginning of words.

gulp

wand

I Write *lp* or *nd* to finish each word.

a wi__________

b ki__________

c ba__________

d gu__________

e ha__________

f la__________

g pu__________

h he__________

i fi__________

j sa__________

II Draw a line to match the *lp* and *nd* words to the pictures.

a band b hand c yelp d help e gulp

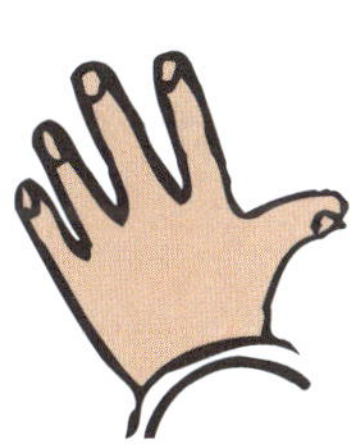

Words using *st*

The letters *s* and *t* appear in many words to make the blend *st*.

stamp po**st**age po**st**

I Tick the word in each pair that ends in *st*.

a	post	☐	pole	☐
b	pick	☐	last	☐
c	blast	☐	plate	☐
d	fake	☐	fast	☐
e	just	☐	jump	☐

f	bin	☐	bust	☐
g	trust	☐	take	☐
h	make	☐	must	☐
i	beast	☐	drink	☐
j	least	☐	lady	☐

II Choose the correct *st* word, so the sentences make sense. Cross out the word you do not need.

a There was **dust mast** everywhere.

b I used **yeast dust** to make my bread.

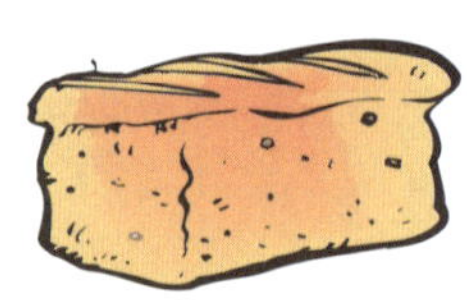

c I like history because you learn about the **past crust**.

d The sail flew from the **mast feast**.

e I **must mast** try harder!

f Mum made us a tasty **past feast**.

g I like the **dust crust** on the bread best.

ee words

The letters *ee* together sound like someone is squealing!

I Draw a line to match each *ee* word to the right picture.

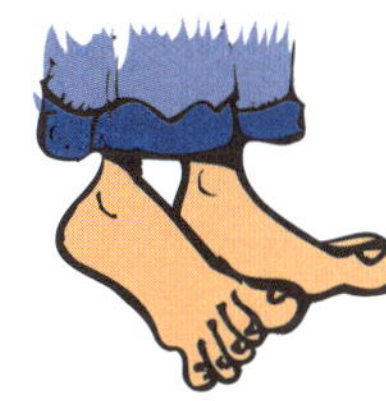

a sleep
b sheep
c feet
d sleet
e sheet
f beer
g deer
h beep

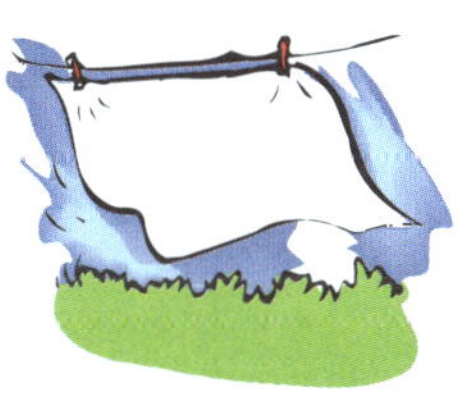

II Draw a circle round the *ee* word in each sentence.

a The water is deep.
b Have you seen my dad?
c Where have you been?
d My sister is a teenager.
e I shall creep up the stairs, because my brother is sleeping.
f Have a peep at these chicks!
g The car horn went beep.
h In the winter we get sleet as well as snow.

oo sounds

oo makes a **special sound**, like an owl hooting.

hoot root soon

I Draw a picture of the missing *oo* words in the boxes below. Use the words in the box to help you.

stool	pool	food	school

a The cat sat on the ________.

b Who would like to swim in the ________?

c The ________ was very noisy!

d What is your favourite ________?

II Write the correct *oo* word in each sentence.

too
moon
wool
cool
spoon

a The ________ was bright in the sky.

b The lemonade was lovely and ________.

c I eat yoghurt with a ________.

d Can I come ________?

e ________ is made into jumpers.

oa words

There are lots of words that use the letters *oa* together. They make a sound like the name of the letter *o*.

boar

toad

I Which pictures are *oa* words? Circle the ones you choose.

a 

b 

c 

d 

e 

f 

II Draw a line to match each *oa* word to its clue.

a toast	it sails on the sea
b foal	cars drive on this
c coal	bread
d loaf	baby horse
e oak	it is like a frog
f boat	it burns on a fire
g toad	a hot, cooked slice of bread
h road	tree

ai words

The letters *a* and *i* blend together to make the sound *ay* – just like a person who has not heard what you said!

I Draw a picture for each *ai* word.

a snail

c brain

e train

b rain

d tail

f nail

II Write a sentence using each *ai* word.

a snail ______________________________

b main ______________________________

c pail ______________________________

d fail ______________________________

e rain ______________________________

f pain ______________________________

ie and *y* words

The letter blend *ie* sometimes makes the same sound as the letter *y* when it is at the end of a word – so it can be confusing!

pie

why

I Which letters are correct? Underline the right answer.

a pie py

b tie ty

c die dy

d ly lie

e thyf thief

f trys tries

g why whie

h flie fly

i cry crie

j by bie

II Complete the words. They all end in *y* or *ie*.

a d______

c cr______

e t______

b fl______

d sp______

Making words

You can **build words** by adding different groups of letters together.

cr + isp = *crisp*

I Add these groups of letters together and write the words you make.

a	th	+	at	=	that	f	wh	+	ip	=	______
b	th	+	is	=	______	g	tr	+	ap	=	______
c	th	+	en	=	______	h	dr	+	op	=	______
d	wh	+	at	=	______	i	cr	+	op	=	______
e	wh	+	en	=	______	j	br	+	an	=	______

II Join together the groups of letters with a line to make words. Use a different colour felt pen for each word.

a	tr	ant
b	pl	ade
c	br	ing
d	bl	it
e	cr	en
f	sm	ab
g	spl	esh
h	dr	ile
i	fr	ip
j	wh	ee

Question marks

Question marks look like this **?**. They are used at the end of a sentence to show it is a question.

Some words give us a clue that a sentence is being asked:

What...? When...? How...?
Why...? Who...?

Where is my hat?

I Add a question mark or a full stop at the end of these sentences.

a Do you like football

b I am glad we are going there

c Can we go now

d May I have one please

e You can play

f This is my dog

g What was that noise

h What time is it

II Write questions of your own using the words what, when, how, why, who. Do not forgot the question mark!

a ______________________________

____

b ______________________________

____

c ______________________________

____

d ______________________________

____

e ______________________________

____

Plurals

Where there is more than one thing, we say it is a **plural**.

To make the word **frog** plural, add an *s*. This shows there is more than one.

one frog

→

two frog**s**

I **Circle all the plural words.**

a The horses eat hay.

b The birds flew away.

c Some girls like swimming.

d The flowers are pretty.

e Have you seen my comics?

f These are my favourite sweets.

g The dogs are barking.

h Would you like some crisps?

II **Some plurals do not add an *s*. Join the word to the plural with a line.**

a woman	mice
b goose	men
c mouse	women
d man	geese
e louse	lice

In the past

When the **action word** in a sentence ends in *ed* it means the action happened in the past.

I walk**ed** to school yesterday.

Some words change completely

I **run** *fast* changes to I **ran** *fast*

I **Change the action word to the past tense. The first one has been done for you.**

a I lik*ed*____ the games best.

b I talk______ to my friend.

c I look______ at the picture.

d She play______ with her brother.

e He paint______ a picture.

f I call______ my sister.

g They wash______ their hands.

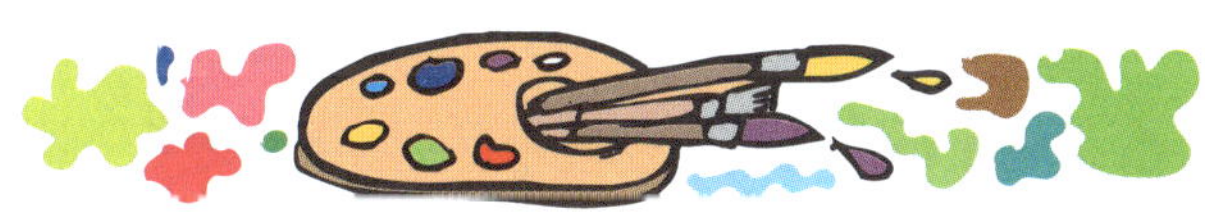

II **Write the correct present tense word next to the past tense word. The first one has been done for you.**

a jumped ___*jump*___

b hopped __________

c tried __________

d called __________

e ran __________

f lifted __________

g skipped __________

h cried __________

i helped __________

run	jump	skip	help	
try	hop	call	cry	lift

Vowels

The letters

a e i o u

are called **vowels**.

Sometimes *y* acts as a vowel in words like 'cry' and 'why'.

Do have some tea.

I Circle the vowels in these words.

a c o t t a g e

b s e a s i d e

c w o o d s

d b a b i e s

e s c h o o l

f c o m p u t e r

g p i c t u r e

h d o c t o r

i b e r r i e s

j l e a f

II Fill in the missing vowels to make these words.

a h_____ _____se

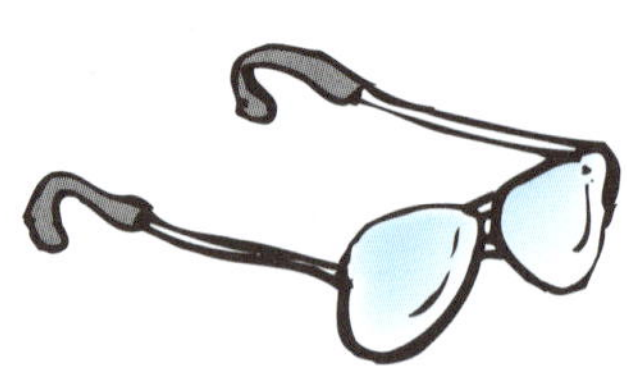

c gl_____ss_____s

e c_____k_____

b b_____ _____ks

d m_____lk

f st_____rs

Consonants

Consonants are all the letters of the alphabet except the vowels *a e i o u*.

The consonants are:

b c d f g h j k l m n p
q r s t v w x y z

I Underline the consonants in these words.

a boat
b baby
c mouse
d sand
e sunshine
f desk
g pencil
h scissors
i envelope
j table

II Write the names of the things under the pictures. Use pairs of consonants in the box to help you.

a 

___a___

b 

___a___

c 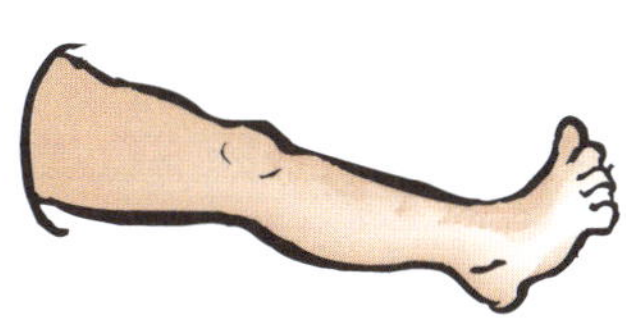

___e___

d 

___a___

e 

___a___

ct	lg	mn
jm	cn	

Same meanings

Sometimes, different words can be used to say the **same thing**.

shout yell roar

These words can all be used to mean someone is talking very loudly.

I What words mean the same thing? Draw a line to link the matching words.

a big	run
b small	blossom
c shiny	loud
d noisy	tiny
e dash	softly
f gently	seat
g flower	sparkly
h chair	huge

II Think of a word that means the same as these words. Write your word in the space.

a smelly	*stinky*	f sad	______
b sleepy	______	g happy	______
c jump	______	h angry	______
d walk	______	i wet	______
e cry	______	j squashy	______

Opposites

Dark and **light** have opposite meanings.

During the day, it is light.

At night, it is dark.

I **Draw a line to match the opposites.**

a open	shiny
b big	shut
c tidy	horrible
d dull	dry
e hard	soft
f wet	quiet
g loud	messy
h lovely	small

II **Think of a word that means the opposite of each of the words below. Write your words in the spaces.**

a happy	sad	f full	________
b awake	________	g slow	________
c out	________	h man	________
d up	________	i run	________
e after	________	j low	________

ANSWERS

Page 2

I
- a fan
- b stink
- c plug
- d red
- e dot
- f sack

II
- a smell
- b park
- c frog
- d fox
- e bin
- f rock
- g pig

Page 3

I
- a a b c d e f g
- b u v w x y z
- c p q r s t u v
- d f g h i j k l m
- e j k l m n o p
- f r s t u v w x
- g d e f g h i j k

II
- a box, cat, egg
- b apple, bag, dig
- c art, cup, pig
- d baby, car, dog
- e bed, door, wall
- f book, leg, sun
- g bird, peg, tree

Page 4

I Spellings remembered.

II
- a man
- b fin
- c pig
- d pin
- e dot
- f wig
- g sun
- h ball

Page 5

I Words overwritten neatly.

II Words copied correctly; rounded letters, correctly formed, sitting on lines.

Page 6

I
- a I like you.
- b This is my sister.
- c Sausages are my favourite.
- d I am going out.
- e I want to read.

II
- a I like my brother.
- b My dog likes walking.
- c The cat can smell its food.
- d We eat sweets.
- e Rain makes you wet.

Page 7

I
- a Brian
- b Mrs Jones
- c Andrew
- d England
- e Mr Brown
- f Miss Lacey
- g London
- h Mr Smith
- i France
- j Janet
- k Doctor Doolittle
- l Cambridge
- m Africa
- n Scotland

II
- a My friend Jamila comes from Yorkshire.
- b My dog is called Bertie.
- c Auntie Jane lives in Edinburgh.
- d Bruce, Stella and Jodi are my friends.
- e We sailed down the River Thames.
- f Dad's name is John.
- g I am going on holiday to Portugal with my sister Sarah.
- h I went to Durham to see the pantomime Cinderella.

Page 8

I
- a fluff
- b puff
- c buff
- d cuff
- e sniff
- f stiff
- g muff
- h stuff
- i staff
- j whiff

II
- a giraffe
- b puff
- c sniff
- d whiff
- e cliff
- f muff

Page 9

I Children will not know all of the words below, but they are given for correctness.
- a ball, bull, bill, bell
- b yell
- c sill, sell
- d call, cell, cull
- e hill, hall, hull, hell
- f doll, dell, dull, dill
- g fall, fill, full, fell
- h pull, pill, pall, poll
- i till, tall, tell, toll
- j will, wall, well

II
- a ball
- b wall
- c bell
- d bull
- e well
- f doll

Page 10

I

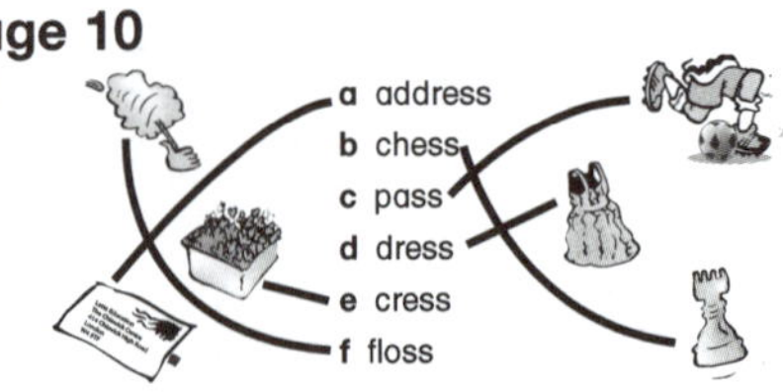

II
- a grass
- b mess
- c cress
- d floss
- e kiss
- f hiss

Page 11

I Check child's pictures of each 'ck' item.

II
- a sick, sock
- b knock
- c wick
- d flick, flock
- e pick, pock
- f Rick, rock
- g lick, lock
- h stick, stock
- i smock
- j trick

Page 12

I
- a rectangle
- b orange
- c orangutan
- d sing
- e king
- f triangle
- g penguin
- h swing
- i ring
- j finger
- k sting
- l herring

II Any reasonable sentences containing the words.

Page 13

I
- a bland
- b black
- c blue
- d blend
- e blank
- f bleat
- g bleep
- h bloat
- i bleak
- j blade

II Check child's pictures of the words listed.

Page 14

I

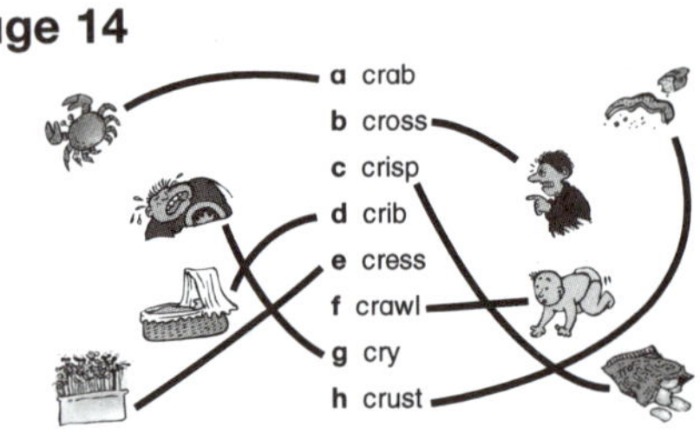

II Check child's pictures of the words listed.

Page 15

I (in any order)
- a trade
- b trip
- c tramp
- d trash
- e true
- f trumpet
- g travel
- h tray

II
- a track
- b tractor
- c train
- d trap
- e traffic
- f tree
- g try